ECHOES OF GOODBYE

Echoes of Goodbye

Verses of Loss and Renewal

ARIA PHOENIX

Dedication

To the hearts wandering in the aftermath of loss,
To those who have felt the cold touch of heartbreak,
And yet, brave the storm in search of their dawn.
This book is a testament to your resilience,
A mirror reflecting the beauty of your strength,
And a reminder that within you lies
The power to heal, to grow, and to love once more.
May these pages be a companion on your journey
Towards the light that awaits beyond the shadows.

FOREWORD

In the intricate tapestry of human experience, heartbreak is a thread that weaves through many of our lives, leaving behind patterns of sorrow, resilience, and ultimately, transformation. It is a universal language, understood by all, yet uniquely experienced by each soul. This book, born from the depths of such universal truths, seeks to explore the nuanced journey from the rawness of heartbreak to the warm embrace of healing.

Each poem within these pages serves as a steppingstone across the tumultuous waters of loss and recovery. They are not just words, but lifelines thrown into the vast sea of our collective emotions, meant to guide, comfort, and inspire. As you navigate through "The Fracture," "The Descent," "The Reckoning," "The Healing," and finally, "The Emergence," you will encounter the shadows of past pains but also the light of newfound wisdom and strength.

This book is an invitation to walk alongside me through the darkest nights and into the breaking dawn. It is a reflection on the beauty of our brokenness and the incredible power of the human spirit to rise, again and again, from the ashes of despair. In sharing this journey, my hope is that you find solace in knowing you are not alone, that your feelings are valid, and that healing is not only possible but inevitable.

Let these poems be a mirror in which you see not just the scars of your past but the promise of your future. May they inspire you to embrace your vulnerabilities, to find strength in your tears, and to recognize that within every ending lies the seed of a new beginning. Heartbreak, after all, is not the end of our story but a pivotal chapter that shapes us, teaches us, and ultimately leads us to the most authentic version of ourselves.

As you turn these pages, remember that the journey of healing is as much about rediscovering who you are as it is about letting go of who you were not meant to be. It is my sincerest wish that, in reading this book, you find the courage to face your own journey with hope, grace, and the unshakable belief that brighter days lie ahead.

Welcome to a journey of healing, of rediscovery, and of love reborn from the ashes of heartbreak. Welcome to your emergence.

CONTENTS

I

The Fracture

II

The Descent

III

The Reckoning

IV

The Healing

V

The Emergence

PART I

THE FRACTURE

PART I: THE FRACTURE

The Last Goodbye

In the silence of our last goodbye,
I found a voice I never knew I had.
The words we never said
echo louder than the ones we did.
In the end,
it was the silence that broke me,
not the goodbye.

PART I: THE FRACTURE

The Moment Everything Changed

In one fleeting moment, our world shifted,
A future once bright turned suddenly muddled and gray.
Words fell like autumn leaves, dry and drifted,
And in their wake, a silence that took my breath away.
The space between us, once warm and tender,
Grew cold and vast as a winter night,
Each unspoken thought a silent surrender,
A white flag raised in our losing fight.

PART I: THE FRACTURE

Unanswered Questions

Why do whispers of love turn to shouts of doubt,
Echoing in chambers of a bewildered heart?
Questions unanswered, a mind in a rout,
Piecing together how we drifted apart.
Was it a word, a look, or a lack thereof,
That tore the fabric of our intertwined souls?
In the aftermath, we're strangers to our love,
A puzzle incomplete, a story full of holes.

PART I: THE FRACTURE

The Echo of Goodbye

Goodbye lingered in the air, a heavy echo, a suffocating veil,
Its weight more than words could ever convey.
It settled in the corners of a life now frail,
A constant reminder that love had gone astray.
Goodbye, a finality we couldn't erase,
A bridge burned down in silent despair.
In its ashes, memories we couldn't replace,
And the haunting realization that you were no longer there.

PART I: THE FRACTURE

Reflections in the Still Water

In the still water, I see a reflection not my own,
A visage marred by sorrow, eyes deep with unshed tears.
The person I knew, now unfamiliar, grown,
Changed by the passage of those relentless years.
Where laughter once danced, now only shadows play,
A canvas of joy now painted over with grief.
In the still water, I see myself every day,
Searching for solace, longing for relief.

PART I: THE FRACTURE

The Art of Losing

To lose is an art, mastered by the unwilling,
A delicate balance of holding on and letting go.
Each memory a brush stroke, vivid and chilling,
Painting a portrait of love's afterglow.
The art of losing isn't hard to master, they say,
Yet each loss leaves a mark, a scar upon the heart.
With every beat, a reminder of the price we pay,
For daring to love, for allowing ourselves to fall apart.

PART I: THE FRACTURE

The Ghost of You

Your ghost wanders through the halls of my mind,
A specter of love, of a time now past.
In every corner, your memory I find,
Haunting the present with shadows cast.
Your laughter echoes, a melody so sweet,
Yet it fades into the silence of the night.
The ghost of you, in every heartbeat,
A reminder of what was, of what might.

PART I: THE FRACTURE

The Space You Left Behind

There's a space where you used to be,
A gap wide as oceans, deep as seas.
I reach out in the darkness, hoping to find,
Something to fill the space you left behind.
But the emptiness echoes back, a stark reply,
A reminder of the void under the starry sky.
In this space, memories flicker and intertwine,
A tapestry of love, in the space you left behind.

PART I: THE FRACTURE

Words Unspoken

Words unspoken, a tale untold,
Linger in the silence, bold and cold.
Words of love, words of pain,
Trapped in the heart, a silent refrain.
If only words could bridge the divide,
Heal the wounds, turn the tide.
But words unspoken remain confined,
A testament to what's left behind.

PART I: THE FRACTURE

The Illusion of Us

We were a mirage, an illusion at best,
A dream conjured in the heart's deep recess.
Believing in us, a folly so grand,
A castle built on shifting sand.
The illusion shattered, a cruel reveal,
Leaving wounds that time may never heal.
In the ruins, a truth so robust,
We were but an illusion, a whisper of dust.

PART I: THE FRACTURE

Winter's Embrace

Winter came early, the chill in your gaze,
Frost on the windowpane of our days.
Love's warm summer, a distant memory,
As cold winds whisper of a love that used to be.
In winter's embrace, we lost our way,
The warmth of our hearts led astray.

PART I: THE FRACTURE

A Symphony of Silence

Our love was a symphony, now fallen quiet,
Notes scattered, melody broken, a riot
Of silence so loud, it drowns out the past,
A future we thought was meant to last.
In the void, the silence composes its tune,
A haunting refrain under the crescent moon.

PART I: THE FRACTURE

The Lighthouse

You were the lighthouse in my tempest sea,
Guiding me home, a beacon of hope to me.
But the light dimmed, the seas grew rough,
The storms of life, relentless and tough.
Now adrift in darkness, no light to see,
Wondering if a lighthouse you ever were to me.

PART I: THE FRACTURE

Tides of Farewell

The tides pull us apart, a farewell so sweet,
Waves of memories, moments we can't repeat.
Each ebb and flow, a reminder so cruel,
Of love's fleeting moments, its unspoken rule.
In the tides of farewell, we find our release,
Surrendering to the currents, in search of peace.

PART I: THE FRACTURE

The Chasm

Between us, a chasm, wide and deep,
Filled with words we could not speak.
Once bridged by love, now a void so vast,
A testament to a love that couldn't last.
In the chasm's depths, our whispers die,
Echoes of a love, beneath the open sky.

PART I: THE FRACTURE

Shadows of Doubt

Shadows of doubt, creeping in,
Dimming the love that once had been.
In their wake, a trail of fears,
Unspoken thoughts, unshed tears.
Shadows growing, day by day,
Until our love faded away.

PART I: THE FRACTURE

The Hourglass

Our love, an hourglass, grains of sand so fine,
Moments slipping through, no longer mine.
Time, relentless, eroding our shore,
Leaving behind memories, nothing more.
As the last grain falls, I understand,
Our love, but a moment, a grain of sand.

PART I: THE FRACTURE

The Portrait

A portrait of love, now hanging askew,
Colors fading, a change in the hue.
Once vibrant shades of joy and desire,
Now muted, consumed by time's fire.
In the portrait's gaze, a silent plea,
A memory of what used to be.

PART I: THE FRACTURE

Shadows at Noon

In the glaring light of the noonday sun,
Shadows lengthen, subtly spun.
An ironic twist of fate, it seems,
Where light is brightest, darkness gleams.

We walked together, hand in hand,
Shadows merging with the land.
But as the sun reached its peak,
Our shadows faltered, grew weak.

Your shadow drifted, began to fade,
As if it sought a different shade.
Left behind, mine stood alone,
A dark silhouette, fully grown.

In this brightness, why do I feel cold?
Our story of love, barely old.
The sun burns, yet I'm chilled within,
A paradox of warmth, a love grown thin.

Yet, in this moment, stark and clear,
A truth emerges, drawing near.
That even at noon, shadows fall,
And in absence, I stand tall.

For shadows prove the light exists,
Despite the pain, love persists.

So, I'll embrace the shadow and the gleam,
For both are parts of this life's dream.

    In every shadow, at every noon,
Lies the promise of a new moon.
Where darkness reigns, stars shine bright,
Guiding me through the longest night.

PART I: THE FRACTURE

The Turning of Seasons

Love, like seasons, turns in its time,
From the warmth of summer to winter's cold rhyme.
We blossomed in spring, flourished in sun,
But as autumn arrived, our unraveling begun.
Leaves fell, and so did we,
From the heights of love, from an us that was free.

Winter's chill wrapped around our embrace,
Silent frost upon morning's face.
Gone were the nights under starlit skies,
Replaced by whispers, by cold goodbyes.
In the heart of winter, love seemed lost,
Buried under frost, under snow's soft gloss.

Yet, as all seasons, winter too shall pass,
Snow will melt, revealing green grass.
Beneath the cold, life patiently waits,
For warmth to return, to open the gates.
And though our love like autumn leaves did fall,
The spring ahead holds new love, after all.

For seasons turn, and with them, so do hearts,
What once was ended, again restarts.
The cycle of love, of loss, of pain,
Is but a journey, with much to gain.
As seasons change, so do we grow,
Learning to love, to let go, to glow.

In the turning of seasons, we find our way,
Through the coldest nights, into brighter day.
Though love may wane like the waning year,
New beginnings, like spring, always draw near.
So, we cherish each season, each moment of sun,
For in the turning of seasons, life's tapestry is spun.

PART II

THE DESCENT

PART II: THE DESCENT

Reflections in the Dark

I searched for you in others,
finding only fragments
of a love that was never meant
to be whole again.
In the dark,
I learned to love the pieces,
not the whole,
finding peace in the reflection
of my fractured self.

PART II: THE DESCENT

Nights Without Stars

Nights without stars, dark and deep,
Where lonely whispers and shadows creep.
In this darkness, I find my fight,
Searching for stars, craving the light.

PART II: THE DESCENT

The Weight of Goodbye

Goodbye, a weight, heavy and true,
A burden I carry, in hues of blue.
Each step, a reminder of what I've lost,
Goodbye, a word, too high a cost.

PART II: THE DESCENT

Echoes of You

In the silence, your echoes roam free,
A haunting melody, a locked memory.
With every beat of my heart, I hear,
Echoes of you, painfully clear.

PART II: THE DESCENT

Shattered

Shattered, not like glass on the floor,
But like waves crashing against the shore.
Relentless, raw, a force untamed,
Shattered, but still whole, unnamed.

PART II: THE DESCENT

Invisible Chains

Bound by invisible chains, tight and secure,
To a love that was never pure.
Breaking free, a task so daunting,
These chains, silently haunting.

PART II: THE DESCENT

The Art of Drowning

Learning to breathe, under the weight of pain,
An art of drowning, in the love that remains.
Each breath a struggle, each moment a fight,
Learning to drown, to finally see the light.

PART II: THE DESCENT

Fractured Echoes

In the quiet,
our conversations replay,
fractured echoes of a better yesterday.
Each word a reminder,
each silence a blade,
carving out memories that refuse to fade.

PART II: THE DESCENT

Unseen Wounds

You can't see the wounds,
hidden beneath smiles and routine.
But they bleed in silence,
seeping through cracks unseen.
A heart, quietly breaking,
over what could have been.

PART II: THE DESCENT

Ghosts of Us

Ghosts of us linger in empty rooms,
dancing in the dust,
whispers of laughter and despair,
a love that turned to rust.
I walk among these specters,
haunted by the loss of us.

PART II: THE DESCENT

The Art of Forgetting

Forgetting you
is an art I cannot master,
a skill beyond my grasp.
Memories, stubborn painters,
keep coloring my present
with shades of our past.

PART II: THE DESCENT

Solitary Nights

Solitary nights stretch endlessly,
a universe expanding between my sheets.
Where once you lay, now lies a galaxy
of questions, doubts, and incomplete dreams.

PART II: THE DESCENT

The Weight of Absence

Your absence weighs more
than your presence ever did.
A paradox, heavy with irony,
a heart, burdened by what it now lacks,
learns to carry the weight of being alone.

PART II: THE DESCENT

Drowning in Dry Land

I'm drowning on dry land,
gasping for air in an ocean of emptiness.
Your absence, a void, pulls me under,
a riptide of sorrow in a sea of silence.

PART II: THE DESCENT

Echoes of Goodbye

The echoes of our goodbye
reverberate through the canyons of my mind,
a soundless symphony of closure,
playing to an audience of one.

PART II: THE DESCENT

The Price of Memory

Memories, once treasures,
now tax my soul like curses.
The price of recalling joy
is the sorrow of its absence.

PART II: THE DESCENT

Falling Stars

We were like falling stars,
a spectacular blaze of glory and dreams,
destined to burn out,
leaving darkness in our wake.

PART II: THE DESCENT

The Illusion of Healing

Healing feels like an illusion,
a mirage in the desert of my despair.
With each step forward,
it seems to slip further away,
a trick of the light,
or perhaps of the heart.

PART II: THE DESCENT

Shadows and Dust

Love, now shadows and dust,
a memory fading into the night.
What once burned so bright
leaves only ashes,
carried away by the indifferent wind.

PART II: THE DESCENT

The Silence Between

In the silence between us,
a chasm widens,
filled with words unspoken,
love ungiven,
a bridge, once sturdy,
now lost to the void.

PART III
THE RECKONING

PART III: THE RECKONING

The Turning Point

In the quiet aftermath,
I found the pieces of me you left unclaimed.
Gathering them, I realized
The person you left is not the one to be reclaimed.
This is not a story of loss,
But one of discovery
And the turning point
Where I found myself,
Not as you left me,
But as I am, whole.

PART III: THE RECKONING

The Lesson Learned

Love taught me in its leaving,
The strength found in the depth of pain.
A heart that's broken, still beating,
Learns to love itself again.

PART III: THE RECKONING

Reckoning

There's a reckoning in the quiet,
A confrontation with the soul.
In the mirror of my fears,
I see a vision of me, whole.
Broken, yes, but also new,
Rebuilt from the ash and rue.

PART III: THE RECKONING

Letting Go

Letting go isn't forgetting,
It's remembering without pain.
Holding on to the lesson,
Not the loss, not the chain.
With each breath, I release
A piece of you, finding peace.

PART III: THE RECKONING

Growth

Growth is a journey, not a destination,
Marked by scars, not celebrations.
Each step forward, a story told,
Of warmth rediscovered in the cold.

PART III: THE RECKONING

The Art of Healing

Healing is an art,
Crafted with tears and time.
Each stroke a part
Of a masterpiece, sublime.
Not defined by the hurt that was,
But by the strength that emerges,
And the love that self-love does.

PART III: THE RECKONING

Bridges Not Burned

I've learned to build bridges where I once would burn,
Connecting the lessons from each turn.
The path to forgiveness, a road less traveled,
Is where the threads of healing are unraveled.

PART III: THE RECKONING

Embrace of Solitude

In solitude, I found an embrace,
A quiet space to heal, to face
The parts of me long ignored,
In solitude, I was restored.

PART III: THE RECKONING

Whisper to My Heart

In the silence, a whisper to my heart,
A gentle reminder that to begin,
Sometimes means to part.
In myself, a newfound art,
The beauty of a fresh start.

PART III: THE RECKONING

The Phoenix Rises

From the ashes of what was,
A phoenix rises, not because
It never knew the agony of the flame,
But because it learned to dance in the pain.

PART III: THE RECKONING

The Unseen Strength

Strength isn't always seen,
Often felt in moments between
The breaking and the mending,
Where our spirits are bending,
Not breaking, but instead,
Learning to fly instead of dread.

PART III: THE RECKONING

On Forgiveness

Forgiveness is a gift, not just to the forgiven,
But to the forgiver, a peace to be livin'.
It's not forgetting, but rather, it's setting
A heart free from the netting
Of past hurts and regretting.

PART III: THE RECKONING

The Journey Within

The longest journey, often the one within,
Through the layers of noise, beneath the skin.
Where truth resides, quiet, profound,
In this journey, I am found.

PART III: THE RECKONING

Echoes of Hope

In the darkest night, the faintest echo of hope,
A lifeline, a rope.
Pulling me from the depths, showing me the scope,
Of a life beyond, with strength to cope.

PART III: THE RECKONING

The New Dawn

With each new dawn, a promise made anew,
To love myself, to be true.
Not just to survive, but to thrive,
In the warmth of the sun, I am alive.

PART III: THE RECKONING

Reclaimed

Reclaimed, not just recovered,
A soul once smothered, now uncovered.
In the wreckage of the past,
A future bright, vast.

PART III: THE RECKONING

The Quiet After the Storm

In the quiet after the storm,
A new world, reborn.
Where once there was ruin, now there's form,
In the quiet, I am warm.

PART III: THE RECKONING

The Light Within

There's a light within, once dim, now bright,
Guiding me through the darkest night.
A beacon of self-love, of might,
In this light, I find my flight.

PART III: THE RECKONING

Reflections of Growth

In the mirror, reflections of growth,
A testament to the oath.
To choose healing over loath,
In growth, I find my troth.

PART III: THE RECKONING

The Horizon Calls

The horizon calls, a future bright,
Beyond the trials, beyond the plight.
In this journey, my heart takes flight,
Towards the horizon, into the light.

Where shadows lingered, now there's day,
Guiding my steps, showing the way.
Past pains and sorrows begin to fray,
As the horizon calls, I must not delay.

With every sunrise, a promise made,
Of scars that fade, of debts repaid.
In the warmth of dawn, fears are allayed,
Towards the horizon, I am swayed.

Through stormy seas and darkest night,
I've held on with all my might.
Now at the brink of newfound sight,
The horizon glows, ever so bright.

Whispers of wind, a gentle plea,
To trust in what I've yet to see.
The horizon calls, to be free,
A journey to what I'm meant to be.

A step forward, into the unknown,
Leaving behind the seeds once sown.

Towards the horizon, how I've grown,
In its light, my true self shown.

    The horizon calls, not just an end,
But a place where heart and soul mend.
With each step, I comprehend,
The journey's worth, the message it sends.

    So I answer the call, with hope anew,
To the horizon, where skies are blue.
A testament to all I've been through,
The horizon calls, and I pursue.

PART IV
THE HEALING

PART IV: THE HEALING

Self-Love

i learned
that healing
is not just about
letting go of the past
but about
falling in love
with myself
for the first time

PART IV: THE HEALING

The Journey Back

the journey back to yourself
is the most magnificent kind of travel
you will undertake
with each step
rediscovering the galaxies
within your soul

PART IV: THE HEALING

Growth

growth is
the slow bloom
after the harshest winter
it's discovering
the strength that was
always rooted
within

PART IV: THE HEALING

Healing Waters

    in the healing waters of solitude
i bathed my soul
washing away the residue
of past hurts
emerging
renewed
and whole

PART IV: THE HEALING

Liberation

i found liberation
in the realization
that i could fill
the empty spaces
within me
with my own love
and not the echoes
of someone else's affection

PART IV: THE HEALING

Stillness

in the stillness
i discovered
the sounds
of my own healing
the beating of a heart
once bruised
now strong
the rhythm
of my breath
a melody
of peace

PART IV: THE HEALING

The Horizon

towards the horizon
i gaze
with eyes wide
and heart open
each step
an affirmation
of my journey
towards healing
and the endless possibilities
that lie ahead

PART IV: THE HEALING

The Fire Within

within me
burns a fire
fueled by resilience
and the ashes
of my past selves
it is this fire
that illuminates
my path forward
and warms
the seeds of my growth

PART IV: THE HEALING

The Dance

life is a dance
of letting go
and holding on
in healing,
i learned
when to step forward
and when to step back
each movement
a step closer
to where i belong

PART IV: THE HEALING

Mosaic

we are mosaics
pieces of light, love, history, stars
glued together with magic and music and words
our healing
a process of arranging
the pieces
into something beautiful

PART IV: THE HEALING

Boundaries

i learned
to build boundaries
not to keep the world out
but to keep my peace in
a sanctuary
within
where i grow
unhindered

PART IV: THE HEALING

Letting Light In

i broke open
not to fall apart
but to let the light in
illuminating the dark corners
of my soul
showing me
the way home

PART IV: THE HEALING

The Quiet After

there is a quiet
that comes after the storm
not the absence of noise
but the presence
of peace
a silence
that heals

PART IV: THE HEALING

Reclamation

i reclaimed
my heart
from the ruins
a phoenix
rising
with each beat
a testament
to survival

PART IV: THE HEALING

Stardust

we are made of stardust
and to the stars
we return
in moments of healing
we shine
reflecting the light
of a thousand suns

PART IV: THE HEALING

The Healing Touch

your own touch
can heal the wounds
left by another
the gentle caress
of self-compassion
mending
what was once broken

PART IV: THE HEALING

The Art of Being

there is an art
to simply being
not mending
not breaking
just existing
in perfect harmony
with the rhythm of the universe

PART IV: THE HEALING

Roots and Wings

from the depths of my despair
i grew roots
anchoring me
to my essence
and from there
i sprouted wings
to fly
towards my rebirth

PART IV: THE HEALING

Wholeness

wholeness isn't found
in the presence of another
it's in the quiet moments
alone
when you realize
you are enough

PART IV: THE HEALING

The Mirror's Truth

I looked in the mirror
and for the first time
I saw clarity
not just the reflection
of who I was
but the promise
of who I could be.

In the glass, a story told in scars,
Each a chapter, not of defeat,
But of battles bravely fought,
And victories hard-won,
A testament to resilience,
To the strength that lies within.

The eyes that met mine held depths
Of sorrow, joy, and wisdom gained,
Not from avoiding the storms,
But from dancing in the rain,
Embracing each drop,
Turning pain into power.

The mirror's truth was more
Than the sum of external parts,
It was the unveiling of a soul
Reborn from its broken shards,
Pieced together with the gold
Of lessons learned and love discovered.

In that moment of revelation,
The reflection transformed,
No longer a prisoner of the past,
But a pioneer of the path forward,
Armed with the knowledge
That true beauty lies
In the imperfections
That make us uniquely ours.

The mirror's truth spoke of change,
A metamorphosis from within,
Echoing the promise that healing
Is not just about mending what was broken,
But celebrating the new whole
That emerges from the fusion
Of past pain and present courage.

I stepped back from the mirror,
A smile breaking like dawn across my face,
For in understanding my reflection,
I found the courage to embrace
The journey of becoming,
Not who I was, but who I am—
A masterpiece in progress,
Crafted by my own hand.

PART V
THE EMERGENCE

PART V: THE EMERGENCE

Rebirth

in the aftermath,
i found my rebirth
not as i was
but as i am meant to be
stronger
wiser
whole

PART V: THE EMERGENCE

Love, Redefined

i learned that love
is not just something you find
but something you are
a light
you don't have to seek
outside yourself

PART V: THE EMERGENCE

Future's Promise

the future no longer terrifies me
for i have seen my darkest nights
and survived
my eyes are open
to the promise
of a new dawn

PART V: THE EMERGENCE

Gratitude

for every heartbreak,
i hold gratitude
each one taught me
my own strength
and brought me closer
to the love i deserve
within myself

PART V: THE EMERGENCE

The Path Forward

    i step forward
not forgetting the past
but carrying its lessons
like stars
guiding me
on my path
to new horizons

PART V: THE EMERGENCE

Whole

i am whole
not because i am unbroken
but because i embraced
each crack
each flaw
and found beauty
in my own imperfection

PART V: THE EMERGENCE

Ready

   i stand at the brink
of something new
heart open, soul bare
ready
to love and be loved
with the wisdom
of the past
lighting my way

PART V: THE EMERGENCE

The Journey Continues

the journey doesn't end here
with healing comes the courage
to dream
to love
to live
unfettered by the past
i move
into the future

PART V: THE EMERGENCE

Blossoming

beneath the rubble
of my broken heart
i discovered
a seed
waiting to blossom
into something beautiful
something new

PART V: THE EMERGENCE

Self-Love's Embrace

wrapped in the embrace
of my own love
i found the greatest comfort
a love that does not falter
does not abandon
a love that is
unconditionally mine

PART V: THE EMERGENCE

The Power of Now

now is all i have
and it is enough
to make dreams
to heal wounds
to love deeply
now is the foundation
on which i build
everything

PART V: THE EMERGENCE

The Art of Letting Go

letting go
is not a one-time act
but a practice
a daily release
of what no longer serves me
making room
for what does

PART V: THE EMERGENCE

Wings Unfurled

with wings unfurled
i soar
above the pain
above the past
into the vast sky
of possibilities
unlimited
unbounded

PART V: THE EMERGENCE

The Dance of Life

life is a dance
and i have learned
to move
with grace
through light and shadow
embracing each step
each turn
with joy

PART V: THE EMERGENCE

Echoes of Joy

in the quiet moments
i hear it
the echoes of joy
a melody that resonates
with the rhythm
of my healed heart

PART V: THE EMERGENCE

A New Chapter

this is not the end
but a beginning
a new chapter
written by my own hand
with words of hope
and pages
of possibilities

PART V: THE EMERGENCE

Love Anew

i open my heart
to love anew
not as a seeker
but as a giver
rich in the love
i found within
ready to share
its abundance

PART V: THE EMERGENCE

Harmony

i have found harmony
between who i was
and who i am
a delicate balance
of past lessons
and future dreams
singing in unison

PART V: THE EMERGENCE

The Light of Change

change is the light
that guides me forward
illuminating the path
to new beginnings
and to the love
that awaits
beyond the fear

PART V: THE EMERGENCE

The Emergence

Emerging from the cocoon of my past,
I am not the same, nor am I vast,
But in this becoming, I am vast,
Something new, unfurling at last.

Through the chrysalis of pain and time,
I've woven silk from sorrow, sublime.
Breaking free, my soul does climb,
From the depths, to heights divine.

In the light of dawn, I find my grace,
A new form, a different face.
Gone are the shadows, without a trace,
In their stead, a glowing embrace.

I stretch my wings, still wet with dew,
Glistening in the morning's hue.
The world anew, from this view,
Colors bright, and life anew.

The air, it carries a hopeful song,
A melody I've sought for long.
It sings of places where I belong,
A chorus bold, a call strong.

With every beat of newfound wings,
I rise above forgotten things.
To the sky, my spirit sings,
Of joy and all the morrow brings.

The emergence, a dance of light and shade,
A journey through the barricade.
From the ashes, a foundation laid,
For the life I've now remade.

So here I stand, at the threshold wide,
With open arms and eyes that bide.
The past, a guide by my side,
As I step into the tide.

Of endless skies and dreams unbound,
Where my true self is finally found.
Above the fray, I am crowned,
In the emergence, I am profound.

AFTERWORD

As we reach the final pages of this journey, I find myself pausing to reflect on the paths we've walked together. Through the valleys of heartbreak to the peaks of healing, each poem has been a step, a breath, a heartbeat in the process of becoming whole again.

This collection was born from the depths of personal experience, yet it has grown beyond me, reaching out to touch the hearts of those who have known loss, who have faced the darkness and dared to seek the light. If these words have found a place in your heart, then know they were meant for you, a beacon in the night guiding us toward a dawn of our own making.

Healing is not a destination but a journey, one that we navigate with resilience and hope. It is my deepest wish that within these pages, you found a reflection of your own strength, a whisper of the possibility that lies within your pain, and the courage to embrace the beauty of your imperfections.

The journey does not end here. With every end comes a new beginning, a chance to rediscover love—in others, in the world, and most importantly, in ourselves. May we all find our way, illuminated by the light of our own emerging dawn.

ACKNOWLEDGEMENTS

This book, a labor of love and healing, would not have come to fruition without the support of many. To those who have walked beside me, both in the light and in the shadow, my gratitude knows no bounds.

To my family, for their unwavering belief in me, even when I struggled to believe in myself. Your love has been my anchor and my guide.

To my friends, who have seen me at my lowest and still chose to sit beside me in the darkness, thank you for your companionship, your laughter, and your unwavering support. You reminded me that even in our most broken moments, we are not alone.

To the countless poets and writers who have inspired me, from the classics to the voices of today, thank you for lighting the way with your words, for showing me the power of poetry to heal, to unite, and to uplift.

To my editor, whose keen eye and gentle guidance helped shape these raw emotions into the collection you hold today. Your patience and insight have been invaluable.

To the readers, who have given these words life beyond the page, thank you for embarking on this journey with me. Your connection to this work completes it, transforming individual experience into universal resonance.

And finally, to anyone who has ever loved and lost, who has been broken but continues to search for the light, this is for you. May we all find our path through the night, guided by the stars of our own making.

Thank you, from the bottom of my heart, for being part of this journey.

www.ingramcontent.com/pod-product-compliance
Lightning Source LLC
Chambersburg PA
CBHW022007170726
47994CB00023B/2419